Powerful, Pleasurable Poetry

Powerful, Pleasurable Poetry

Cover photo: Lake Wanaka, New Zealand by Eric Abalos

Powerful, Pleasurable Poetry

Shelley Meadows

Edited by Stanley J. St. Clair

Powerful, Pleasurable Poetry

© 2017 by Shelley Meadows,
St. Clair Publications

All rights reserved. No part of this publication may be reproduced or transmitted in any form by any means, electronic or mechanical, including telecopy, recording, or any information storage and retrieval system now known or invented, without permission in writing from the publisher, except by a reviewer who wishes to quote brief passages in connection with a review written for inclusion in a magazine, newspaper or broadcast.

ISBN **978-1-935786-49-8**

Printed in the U.S.A

St. Clair Publications

P.O. Box 726

McMinnville, TN 77110-0726

http://stclairpublications.com

Powerful, Pleasurable Poetry

CONTENTS

Soul	7
Just Because	8
Confusion	9
Life	10
Family	11
Trust	12
My Heart	13
Love	14
Lost out of Love	15
Don't Look Back	16
Hope	17
A Boulder	18
God Created a Shelley	19
Hallelujah	20
Pain	21
Just another Day	22
Pain	23

Powerful, Pleasurable Poetry

The Unknown	24
Too Far	25
Grave	26
Time	27
Take a Walk	28
Longing	29
Free	30
About the Poet	31

Soul

I walk in company all the time within shadows I find.

Deep include with a non-free fearful mindset life taking place every step.

Verbally, physically, spiritually on loud creative tones now pleasures unfold.

Never alone, never alone me say, you say, They say, them say, he say, she say, us say, How say, when say, where say, it say, all say, I say feel, I say SOUL.

Just Because

I awoke and began to say, Thank You Lord for this day.

I get dressed and do errands and smile and greet others along the way.

Just because

I am in my home and never alone; feelings of love from up above. I say thank You Lord.

Just because

As I meditate on the good and the bad and the sad, the rich and the poor and the hardships

That have got to be endured, I say Thank You Lord.

Confusion

My mind is in a whirlwind;

I have lost family and friends.

Times as if I was coming and going in a daze;

A mixture of happy and sad, the good and the bad.

Things I know that are real and at the same time an illusion.

In life, we all go through confusion.

Powerful, Pleasurable Poetry

Life

A heartbeat, a breath to take, eyes to awake;

Legs to move, a mouth to speak, a spirit inside to keep us meek.

The joys, the pain, the laughter in the rain

The hardship, the discipline, the peace of happiness.

The sun, the night, a couple; husband and children and wife.

Love, Love, Love,

That is nice for God to give his Son.

Thank you, God, for life

Family

A tie that bonds a relationship that's unbreakable;

A unit filled with the ups and downs, love and anguish —

These emotions are inescapable.

People that stand together no matter what;

The connection that overflows the love cup.

Family, whether right or wrong, with the good Lord's strength;

May it continue with a strong grip —

Family.

Trust

It is an emotion that one must earn;

No longer faking to cause concerns.

Through tough times it lets you know who cares;

The person shows their dedication by always being there.

Trust is a strong bond between people that helps them to connect,

Like a ship that has a link and others just sink;

A tug boat that lets out steam,

Trust makes people a team.

My Heart

My heart has felt so many things.

At times, I want to fly just by a flap of my wings.

I have been strong and weak, too;

Some days happy and feeling blue.

My heart, the part of me no one knows but him and I.

We know the treasures inside that are not on display;

They're not given in vain to be slain.

God has the key and I know it is secure without being abused.

My heart is for giving and receiving love in the right way.

God gives this to me and I to him all day.

My heart

Love

Love is like a battlefield;

You must fight to prove what is real,

The joy and pain; that is the deal.

Some loves grow and others get killed;

Love is what makes the world go around.

God gave us the first love when he sent his Son down.

Why can't we share it with each other? It is a must.

The sickness, how it is misused is a disgust.

Love, stay around; we need you so we won't drown in selfishness.

Save us, love.

Lost out of Love

I begin to look around for a friend and there is no one in sight.

It hurts my soul and I'm disgusted with all my might.

I can`t find what used to sooth and move me;

The lost out of love, it seems gone and set free.

Lost out of love, where could you be?

Then a voice says: My child I've been here, very patiently for you to receive, open up

and breath my love; I never leave.

Don't Look Back

Don't look back in times that family and friends are not around and it is hard;

Don't look back, 'cause pain and confusion seem like they're taking charge.

Don't look back, all is forgotten, the past is behind; the Spirit of God is intertwined.

Don't look back, all we need is God on our minds.

Hope

A feeling so strong that you can't go wrong;

A vision ahead of you that powers your spirit and strengthens every step;

A new person within that lets you know that you are on your way to a journey of happiness and peace.

Thank God for Hope.

A Boulder

I walk around with darkness and sound.

Whatever I can't see the spirit moves me around.

My steps are slower than before; my boulder at times puts me on the floor.

Right when I feel I am going to tap out; my God lightens my boulder off my shoulder.

God shows up on time and lets me know,
My Child and I will always lighten your load.

A long View

As a child, I looked across the meadows and didn't see anything—a view of the land.

Years went by and my eyes saw things that made me happy and cry.

Past, Present and Future has groomed me to be the best child in God as possible.

What God made old, He can make new; that is what I see in the long view.

God Created a Shelley

God could have made me a rabbit with a cotton tail.

God could have made me a reindeer with a bell.

God could have made me a flower to smell.

God could have made me a letter, like the letter L.

God created everything — the heaven and the earth.

God knew I was coming way before my birth.

I am glad that he created my beautiful eyes, my thick thighs, a unique smile a godly conversation that is worthwhile, with dignity and style; yeah, a Shelley.

Hallelujah

When things get tough and stressed, and I know I am doing my best

I say Hallelujah!

Things get very confusing and it feels like I am losing,

I say Hallelujah!

The trials of life don't seem right, and I begin to wrestle with thoughts at night,

I say Hallelujah!

I say Hallelujah and give God the highest praise; to him I am enslaved

Hallelujah!

Just another Day

Just another day to see the trees;

Just another day to work hard and roll up my sleeves;

Just another day to stop and smell the roses;

Just another day to humble ourselves and pray for one another; and to God be the glory.

Just another day for us to tell of love, the godly story.

Pain

I feel uneasy inside that won't let me rest.

It seems at times it's hard for me to take a breath.

This emotion is uncomfortable to the depth of my soul;

That is a story untold.

Here in life we've all got pain for growth and direction.

Our God suffers pain for us to have a sense of protection and his undying love and affection.

The Unknown

In life we all hit the unknown:

A loss for words, an uncertainty on our path.

A strong sense of confusion; a darkness--like a grasp a hold of the past.

A loneliness that weighs you down, that feels like it has no sound.

God is always close to the weary and sad,

Wounded and brokenhearted
through the unknown.

God gave his Son and that's enough love shown

To help us through the unknown.

Too Far

You know I am a child of God and you treat me like I am not.

If I were nothing and had no self-worth, God would not allow my birth.

You look in my eyes and there are no lies inside.

I know I am the apple of his eye and a star; God knows some things go too far.

Grave

Hey, sisters and brothers; are you in a grave in dirt, having no value combined in self-worth?

The smile is not real; with love just a façade to eliminate what's really ill.

Death on the breath, beauty, and longevity and more.

Taste it and see; life is eternity.

Time

The substance that doesn't stand still;

It's always moving out of our control — and will.

Time always repeats itself and begins another day;

While it relapses, changes things in a whole new way.

Time doesn't wait for anyone.

Please don't waste it in your life.

Make every second count alone, husband or wife.

Time…

Take a Walk

As I move through this world not knowing where I will be

My footsteps will not be repeated for me to see…

TAKE A WALK

Each day that passes me by is more knowledge to carry and embrace;

To place upon God and hold his hand for us to talk

With love and compassion in my heart from the Lord God as we take a walk.

Longing

People go through their lives yearning for something inside;

A longing that lingers within that people try to hide

In conversations one will never know

One has it so together that it won't show

A hunger, thirst, carving one carries deep like one is in morning.

These emotions are someone that is longing.

Free

In our world, we are not tied to obligations

Regardless of the right and wrong of our nation

The thoughts our speech can flow without restraint;

Our choices and movements that are quaint

Moving around like the wind to and FRO;

A powerful spirit, within a glow;

No restriction of you and me being free.

Powerful, Pleasurable Poetry

About the Poet, in her own words:

"I am a country girl born in Arkansas who loves my God. These poems will enrich your soul and heart and others that you share them with."

www.ingramcontent.com/pod-product-compliance
Lightning Source LLC
Chambersburg PA
CBHW061316040426
42444CB00010B/2671